Original title:
The Love Lens

Author: Eliora Lumiste
ISBN HARDBACK: 978-9916-86-599-6
ISBN PAPERBACK: 978-9916-86-600-9
ISBN EBOOK: 978-9916-86-601-6

Heartstrings in Focus

In shadows cast by gentle light,
Soft whispers echo through the night.
A melody of hope so near,
Resonates with every tear.

Fragments of dreams dance in the air,
Held close to hearts that deeply care.
The pulse of love draws us near,
A symphony for all to hear.

Eyes meet like stars in the sky,
Bound by a truth we can't deny.
With every heartbeat, love’s embrace,
Sets the rhythm of our pace.

Through tangled paths, our spirits soar,
Navigating what’s at the core.
The language spoken without sound,
In every loss, new love is found.

As heartstrings tug with tender grace,
Each moment shared we shall embrace.
In focus, love’s bright, guiding light,
Reminds us all that we are right.

Landscapes of Longing

Across the hills where shadows play,
Echoes of memories drift away.
A canvas stretched with colors bold,
Tells tales of love, both new and old.

Beneath the trees where silence grows,
Secrets of yearning gently flow.
Touched by the breeze that carries dreams,
Each moment whispers, or so it seems.

In twilight's glow, the heart expands,
While footprints trace along the sands.
The horizon calls with gentle sighs,
As hearts awaken, under wide skies.

With every sunset, colors blend,
Yearning for a distant friend.
In dreams we wander, far and wide,
Through landscapes where our hearts abide.

A river courses, wild and free,
Binding the past to what shall be.
In the vastness, we find our way,
Through landscapes of longing each day.

The Clarity of Embrace

In moments hushed, where silence speaks,
The warmth of love, it softly seeks.
A heartbeat shared amidst the still,
Awakens hope, and bends the will.

With eyes that meet in tender light,
We find a peace that feels so right.
Each sigh exchanged, a melody,
A dance of souls, you and me.

Emotions flowing like a stream,
In clarity, we find our dream.
Every whisper, a gentle grace,
Wraps us in a sweet embrace.

Together we navigate the night,
Guided by love’s eternal light.
In every challenge, hand in hand,
With clarity, together we stand.

As dawn breaks wide, the shadows flee,
Our hearts entwined in harmony.
In love’s embrace, we find our place,
The clarity that time won't erase.

Depth of Affection's Focus

In the quiet hours, we stand still,
Hearts beating softly, a gentle thrill.
Whispers of comfort, shadows drawn close,
Every glance shared, affection engrossed.

A tapestry woven, threads of the past,
Moments of laughter, too bright to cast.
Love’s tender essence, a warm embrace,
In these soft echoes, we find our place.

Hues of Yearning

In twilight's glow, dreams paint the sky,
Colors of longing, a soft lullaby.
Each shade reveals what words cannot say,
In the palette of night, we drift away.

With every heartbeat, passion ignites,
A canvas of wishes, where hope takes flight.
The strokes of emotion, bold yet true,
In the hues of yearning, I find you.

Bokeh of Memory

Fleeting moments, softly blurred,
In frames of laughter, love unheard.
Bokeh glimpses of days gone by,
Captured in stillness, while time flies high.

Each glance a reminder of joy and pain,
A dance of shadows, a sweet refrain.
In the heart's gallery, memories gleam,
A soft-focus dream, forever we dream.

Echoes Through Glass

Through fragile panes, the world has turned,
Reflections of life, where lessons are learned.
Echoes of laughter, whispers of tears,
A resonance forming, through all our years.

The light filters down, casting its spell,
In every shimmer, stories to tell.
The glass glass is thin, yet it holds so much,
In our fleeting moments, love's gentle touch.

Cherished Vistas

In the morning light we rise,
Mountains whisper soft goodbyes.
Golden fields beneath the sky,
Nature's beauty passes by.

Waves that crash upon the shore,
Echo tales of days before.
Footprints left in sands of time,
Memories in rhythm and rhyme.

Breezes carry scents of spring,
Songs of joy that nature sings.
Trees embrace the setting sun,
In this moment, we are one.

Stars emerge in velvet night,
Guiding us with gentle light.
Dreams take flight on wings of hope,
In these vistas, we will cope.

Cherished moments, hearts entwined,
In the tapestry of time.
Every glance and every smile,
Holds the world for just a while.

Scenes from the Heart

Painted hues of love's embrace,
Every touch, a sacred space.
Whispers soft as morning dew,
In this scene, it's me and you.

Candles flicker, shadows dance,
In the night, we take a chance.
Laughter echoes through the halls,
As the night around us calls.

In the garden, blooming bright,
Every flower a shared delight.
Colors blend and scents combine,
In this moment, you're all mine.

Swaying leaves in evening's glow,
Tales of love and dreams we sow.
Memories like petals flow,
In the heart, their warmth will grow.

From the canvas, life draws near,
Every shading holds us dear.
Scenes unfold with every glance,
In the heart, we find our chance.

Weaver of Memories

Threads of laughter, threads of tears,
Woven tightly through the years.
Every stitch a story told,
In the fabric, rich and bold.

Moments captured, times we shared,
In this tapestry, we dared.
Colorful tales of joy and pain,
In the weave, love will remain.

Gentle hands that spin and tuck,
Create a world where we feel luck.
Textures rough and soft caress,
In this art, we are blessed.

Memories fold like paper cranes,
Soaring high, despite the rains.
Crafted dreams in every hue,
Life's great weave, just me and you.

As the loom spins night and day,
We create our own pathway.
Weaver of the heart's delight,
In our memories, dreams take flight.

The Palette of Us

Colors blend in twilight's hush,
Every shade a silent hush.
Brushes dance with tender grace,
Creating dreams, a warm embrace.

Strokes of blue and golden light,
Paint our souls both bold and bright.
In this canvas, hearts align,
Magic flows in every line.

Splashes red of passion's flame,
Yellow hues that call your name.
Green of nature's vibrant song,
In this palette, we belong.

Textures whisper on the page,
In this art, we'll never age.
Every color holds a story,
In our hearts, we find the glory.

As the night brings forth the stars,
We create our blend of ours.
In this masterpiece, we trust,
Together, we are vibrant dust.

Focused on Forever

Time stands still in your gaze,
Every moment, a soft embrace.
Stars whisper their bright truths,
Together, we dance in youth.

Dreams weave through our shared nights,
Guiding us to brilliant heights.
With each step, we carve our way,
Our love grows stronger each day.

In the dark, your light shines clear,
Chasing away every fear.
Like a flame, it brightly glows,
In your warmth, my spirit grows.

Moments captured, hearts entwined,
In this journey, souls aligned.
Focused on the bonds we share,
In forever, we find our prayer.

Pages turned with gentle care,
Each memory a love affair.
With you, time has no end,
Focused on forever, my friend.

Framing Our Journey

Paths we walk with open hearts,
Every step, artful parts.
Together we frame our way,
In life’s canvas, joy's display.

Through valleys low and mountains high,
Hand in hand, we touch the sky.
Each moment, a brush of fate,
Crafting dreams that await.

Colors blend in vibrant hues,
Painting life with vibrant clues.
Together, we’re never lost,
In each other, we found our cost.

Maps unfurl, our spirits soar,
Hurdles faced, we crave for more.
With laughter shared and tears embraced,
Our journey’s framed in love’s grace.

Captured still in every glance,
Life's a beautiful dance.
Framing our journey, side by side,
In this love, forever we’ll abide.

Portraits of Passion

Brush strokes wild on canvas bare,
Each emotion laid out with care.
In colors bright, our story's told,
Portraits of passion that never grow old.

With every line, our hearts entwined,
In laughter's echo, our souls aligned.
Shadows dance in the fading light,
Creating depth in the quiet night.

Captured moments, fleeting yet grand,
In every heartbeat, we understand.
Art of love, both fierce and soft,
In your embrace, I drift aloft.

Frames adorned with shared delight,
Every glance, a memory bright.
Portraits of passion, bold and free,
In your eyes, my world I see.

With vibrant dreams, we brush the skies,
In the masterpiece, our love lies.
Forever cherished, never apart,
These portraits reflect our open heart.

Clarity of the Heart's Eye

In silence, I see your truth,
Reflecting back my deepest youth.
Every heartbeat, a pure refrain,
Clarity found in love's domain.

With each breath, a gentle sigh,
In your gaze, the world feels nigh.
Thoughts converge like rivers flow,
In the heart's eye, love does grow.

Lines of fate drawn in the dark,
In your presence, I find my spark.
Moments merge in a soft light,
Guiding me through the longest night.

Bound by dreams, we'll never stray,
In the heart's eye, we find our way.
Truth unveiled with each soft tear,
Clarity shines, my love is here.

Reflections dance on tender skin,
In the heart's eye, we begin.
Through every trial, we will stand,
With clarity, we hold love's hand.

Fragments of Passion

In whispers soft, our secrets dwell,
In shadows cast, we weave our spell.
With every glance, a spark ignites,
In tender dreams, we soar to heights.

A fleeting touch, a breathless sigh,
Beneath the stars, just you and I.
Where starlit paths entwine our fates,
In passion's dance, our love awaits.

In fragments held, our stories bloom,
A symphony within this room.
With every heartbeat, magic flows,
In every pause, our longing grows.

The world grows dim, our colors bright,
As shadows fall, we claim the night.
In passion's grip, we find our peace,
In fervent hearts, our love won't cease.

A Gaze Beyond Time

In distant realms where dreams unite,
Your eyes hold worlds, both dark and bright.
A fleeting moment, eternity,
In every blink, a memory.

With tender glances, journeys start,
A silent promise, soul to heart.
Across the years, our spirits dance,
In boundless time, we find our chance.

The sands of time in whispers fall,
Yet in your gaze, I feel it all.
From present days to futures bold,
A story of love continues told.

In timeless ways, we write our verse,
In every line, we gently immerse.
With hands entwined, we'll face the storm,
In love's embrace, forever warm.

The Spectrum of Us

In colors bright, our hearts collide,
A vibrant pulse, where dreams reside.
Each hue a tale, a love so true,
In every shade, I see us two.

Through shades of blue and fiery red,
In every glance, words left unsaid.
With laughter's gold and shadows' gray,
In life's embrace, we find our way.

The prism bends, our souls ignite,
In every touch, pure delight.
A dance of colors, night and day,
In every moment, come what may.

With every heartbeat, a vibrant sound,
In love's vast spectrum, we are found.
A canvas vast, we paint our trust,
In shades of hope, in love, we must.

Love in Focus

In the lens of life, we find our way,
Each snapshot tells what words can't say.
In every frame, a story blooms,
In whispered hopes, our love consumes.

With flashes bright, emotions rise,
In captured moments, truth belies.
In every smile, a spark ignites,
In love's own lens, we chase the lights.

The world in focus, blurred edges fade,
In tender smiles, our fears are laid.
Through viewfinders, we start to see,
The beauty in our tapestry.

With colors rich and shadows deep,
Through love’s lens, our memories keep.
A snapshot here, a moment there,
In love's embrace, we have no care.

Through the Aperture of Dreams

In quiet spaces where whispers dwell,
Light streams softly, casting a spell.
Each moment held, a fleeting time,
Captured within the mind's sweet rhyme.

Glimmers of hope, like stars at night,
Guide our hearts in their gentle flight.
Through shadows long, we dare to soar,
Unlocking doors to dreams of yore.

With every breath, the visions dance,
In colors bright, we take a chance.
The world unfolds, a canvas wide,
Through the aperture, where dreams reside.

Pictures of Us

In frames of laughter, in flickers of light,
Moments frozen, forever in sight.
We paint the canvas with every embrace,
Pictures of us, time cannot erase.

Through destinies drawn, hand in hand,
We wander freely, across the land.
Each snapshot a story, a piece of our heart,
Together we thrive, never apart.

The laughter echoes in memories bright,
As we capture the day, and cherish the night.
In every photo, a tale to unfold,
Pictures of us, worth more than gold.

The Film of Forever

Flickering scenes on an endless reel,
Moments entwined, emotions we feel.
In shadows and light, our story is spun,
The film of forever, we're never done.

Through trials we face, our spirits ignite,
In every frame, we find our right.
A love that blossoms, a dance that flows,
As time slips gently, our passion grows.

The final cut captured, a heart's design,
In the cinema of life, your hand in mine.
With every rewind, we cherish the past,
The film of forever, a love built to last.

Connection in Frames

In every glance, electric delight,
Two souls interwoven, a beautiful sight.
Framing the moments, so precious, so rare,
Connection in frames, beyond compare.

With whispers of warmth, our spirits align,
Creating a tapestry, tender and fine.
Captured in stillness, a promise anew,
Connection in frames, it always feels true.

Through echoes of laughter, we weave our design,
Building a world where our hearts intertwine.
In the gallery of life, we find our own place,
Connection in frames, a love we embrace.

Seeing You Clearly

In shadows deep, I find your trace,
Your laughter dances, a warm embrace.
The world stands still, as time unwinds,
In every glance, a truth that binds.

With every smile, the clouds disperse,
You paint my heart, a vibrant verse.
Through stormy skies, your light remains,
A gentle calm amidst the pains.

In tangled thoughts, your name resounds,
With every heartbeat, love astounds.
A mirror's edge, reflections pure,
I see you clearly, forever secure.

So take my hand, let's walk this path,
Through whispered dreams, we'll find our math.
The cosmos sings, a sweet refrain,
With you beside me, joy unchained.

The Artistry of Us

Two souls entwined, a canvas true,
With strokes of fire in every hue.
We craft a world, beyond the gray,
In the artistry, we shape our play.

Your whispers spark, a brush's glide,
In the gallery where our hearts reside.
Each moment splashed, with love's pure glow,
Together we bloom, like flowers grow.

Hands interlaced, we sketch the dreams,
In laughter's chorus, our spirit beams.
The masterpiece that time has made,
An endless tale that won't soon fade.

In every glance, a brush of care,
A tapestry, a love laid bare.
Together, we're the art divine,
In timeless beauty, you are mine.

Quivering Hues of Desire

In twilight's glow, your eyes alight,
A tapestry woven, purest sight.
With every glance, the sparks ignite,
Our secret dance, a sweet delight.

The fragrant blooms of spring's embrace,
Remind me of your gentle grace.
Each whispered word, a soft caress,
In quivering hues, our hearts confess.

With summer's heat, the passion swells,
In silent nights, we weave our spells.
Your touch ignites, the fire we crave,
In moonlit dreams, our desires wave.

As autumn leaves begin to fall,
Our spirits rise above it all.
In every season, heartbeats dance,
In quivering hues, we find romance.

Under the Soft Lens

Beneath the stars, a world unveiled,
In soft focus, our love’s impaled.
With every heartbeat, the colors blend,
A portrait painted, where wonders mend.

Through quiet nights, the shadows sigh,
In gentle hues, our dreams comply.
The echoes whisper, secrets told,
In tender moments, we’re never old.

Your laughter dances, a melody sweet,
In every heartbeat, where we meet.
With every glance, the magic swells,
Under the soft lens, our heart compels.

Let time freeze here, just for a while,
In your embrace, I find my smile.
Under the soft lens, love's embrace,
In every moment, a sacred place.

A Gaze Through Softened Edges

A whisper dances in the air,
Soft light bathes the world with care.
Gentle shadows softly blend,
Transforming shapes where dreams extend.

Each moment, tender yet so frail,
Colors fade like a fleeting sail.
In the twilight's warm embrace,
We lose ourselves, time slows its pace.

The edges blur, horizons bend,
In reflections where we transcend.
A gaze—the world is softly framed,
In every glance, our hearts are named.

Amidst the stillness, secrets bloom,
In quiet corners, finding room.
Together caught in a gentle tide,
Through softened edges, we reside.

This ethereal dance, a soft retreat,
In whispers shared, we find our beat.
With softened edges, we will stay,
In the art of love, come what may.

Captured Glances

In fleeting moments, time stands still,
Captured glances, hearts to fill.
A spark ignites with every glance,
Inviting souls to learn the dance.

Eyes meet softly, a world unveiled,
Silent stories, secrets hailed.
A heartbeat quickens, smiles ignite,
In shared silence, day turns to night.

Every glance a thread of fate,
Woven tightly, never late.
In soft exchanges, truth unfurls,
Painting canvases with our worlds.

Through captured moments, dreams unfold,
In whispers shared, our hearts are bold.
Windows to souls, each look a tome,
In glances shared, we find our home.

A tapestry of unspoken trust,
In every gaze, a timeless thrust.
With each fleeting look, love expands,
Uniting hearts, entwining hands.

The Art of Togetherness

In laughter shared, the moments glow,
Sunlight spilling, soft and slow.
In gentle hands, we bridge the space,
Crafting memories with grace.

With every heartbeat, love creates,
A symphony that captivates.
In the hum of life, we find a way,
To weave our dreams into the day.

Side by side, we face the storm,
In each other, safe and warm.
The art of togetherness takes flight,
In darkest hours, we find the light.

Through challenges faced, we grow and mend,
In this portrait, love will never end.
United hearts in chaos and calm,
In togetherness, we find our balm.

In every heartbeat, we learn, we soar,
With arms entwined, we need no more.
The art we craft, forever shines,
In the tapestry of shared designs.

Reflections of the Heart

Mirrored glimpses, soft and clear,
Whispers echoing, drawing near.
In shadows cast by fears we hide,
Reflections show what lies inside.

With every glance, a story's spun,
In still moments, two become one.
Through laughter shared and tears that fall,
In memories made, we conquer all.

The heart, a canvas, vast and wide,
Colors blend where dreams abide.
In silent thoughts and hopes expressed,
In reflections, we find our quest.

Each heartbeat sings a timeless verse,
In the depths, we silently immerse.
In hues of love, we paint the night,
Reflections dance in the soft moonlight.

Together we walk this winding path,
In the echo of love’s warm bath.
As reflections spark in the quiet dark,
We illuminate what lies at our hearts.

Our Shared Canvas

Brushstrokes of laughter fill the air,
Colors blend, a vibrant affair.
Together we paint our dreams bright,
On this canvas, we find our light.

Each hue tells stories of our days,
In gentle whispers, love conveys.
With every stroke, our spirits soar,
Creating memories we can explore.

A tapestry woven with stitches of time,
In every corner, our souls align.
From the darkest shades to the brightest spark,
Our shared canvas, a beautiful arc.

In the quiet moments, we find our peace,
With every glance, our worries cease.
A masterpiece crafted with care,
Forever bound, a love we share.

The Image of Togetherness

In the frame of life, we stand as one,
Through every storm, our hearts have spun.
A picture painted with trust and grace,
In the gallery of time, we find our place.

Each memory a snapshot, crisp and clear,
Candid moments to hold so dear.
With laughter echoing in the air,
Together, we create a world so rare.

Side by side, we write our tale,
Navigating joy, we never fail.
In the art of living, hand in hand,
The image of us is forever grand.

With colors bright, we shade our lives,
Through every challenge, our bond survives.
In the portrait of love, we find our bliss,
An image too perfect, we can't dismiss.

Radiance of Romance

In twilight's glow, our hearts ignite,
With every whisper, we take flight.
Under the stars, our souls entwine,
In this moment, your heart is mine.

The moonlight dances upon your face,
Every glance, a warm embrace.
We lose ourselves in this sweet trance,
In the radiance of our romance.

Every heartbeat is a song anew,
In this melody, it's me and you.
A symphony played beneath the night,
In love's bright glow, everything feels right.

With every touch, the world fades away,
In your arms, I long to stay.
Together we write our love's refrain,
In the radiance of joy, no room for pain.

When Hearts Align

In the silence, our souls connect,
A rhythm so pure, we both reflect.
With every heartbeat, we find our way,
In harmony, we choose to stay.

Beyond the words, our spirits sing,
In the dance of love, we find our wings.
When hearts align, the world feels right,
In this union, we'll shine so bright.

Through trials faced, we stand as one,
In every challenge, we have won.
A constellation of dreams, we draw,
When hearts align, we stand in awe.

Together we journey through night and day,
With boundless love, we find our way.
In the tapestry of time, we entwine,
Forever, my love, when hearts align.

Visions of Togetherness

In the soft dusk light, we walk,
Hand in hand, hearts unbarred.
Whispers blend, a silent talk,
Underneath the evening star.

Laughter dances on the breeze,
Painting dreams in warm hues.
With each step, we're at ease,
The world fades, just me and you.

Moments shared, our spirits entwined,
Like vines beneath the moon's glow.
In this bond, joy is designed,
Together, we'll forever grow.

Through storms that echo and roar,
We'll find shelter in embrace.
Our voices mingling, evermore,
In this timeless, sacred space.

Visions clear, our paths aligned,
In a tapestry of light.
With love's thread, we are confined,
A journey made pure and bright.

The Crystal of Connection

Glimmers spark like distant stars,
In the silence, our souls greet.
Reflections weave, no bounds, no bars,
A dance that feels complete.

Within your gaze, I find my home,
A haven wrapped in grace.
Through every fear and every roam,
Your light becomes my space.

Each word, a gem, so rare and true,
Carving pathways in our minds.
In the vastness, just us two,
Our essence intertwined.

Time suspends, as moments meld,
In laughter's crystal glow.
With every dream, our hearts compelled,
Together, we will flow.

In this sphere, our spirits sing,
Bound by threads of fate.
In the echoes, love will ring,
A crystal bond, innate.

Framed in Desire

A canvas blooms with hues so bright,
Passion strokes, our spirits rise.
Each glance ignites the softest light,
Framed forever in our sighs.

Fingers brush, a spark ignites,
In the dance of the night air.
Whispers linger in the heights,
In a moment, stripped of care.

Painted sunsets, soft and warm,
Where shadows play and dreams roam.
Our hearts beat in a wild swarm,
In this place, we are home.

Every heartbeat, a symphony,
Composed in sweet refrain.
In this art of you and me,
Desire flows like gentle rain.

In the frame, we capture time,
Echoes of a love so real.
With each brush, our hearts in rhyme,
In this desire, we conceal.

Insights of the Heart

Within the stillness, truths emerge,
Words unspoken, yet so clear.
In this silence, love's soft surge,
Whispers of what we hold dear.

Eyes that speak, a language pure,
A glance that crosses the divide.
In your warmth, I feel secure,
In our hearts, dreams coincide.

Moments shared, a tender gaze,
In the quiet, secrets bloom.
Through every trial, through every phase,
Together, we dispel the gloom.

Each heartbeat resonates in time,
A rhythm born of trust and fate.
In this dance, our souls align,
With every step, we elevate.

Insights gathered, wisdom flows,
In the depths of love's embrace.
In this journey, our spirit grows,
With every heartbeat, we find grace.

In the Frame of Affection

In laughter's light, we dance with glee,
Captured moments, just you and me.
Soft whispers weave through the air,
In a world painted pure, kind, and rare.

Every glance a brushstroke made,
In this art, love will never fade.
Gentle echoes of sweet embrace,
Sketching memories time can't erase.

Hands entwined, hearts beating fast,
In this frame, treasures amassed.
A canvas of dreams built so high,
Where every color reflects our sky.

Through storms and sun, we stand our ground,
In this portrait, solace found.
With every stroke, our tale unfolds,
A masterpiece, more precious than gold.

Together we paint, forever entwined,
In this frame, our souls aligned.
With every hue, we draw anew,
In the frame of affection, it's me and you.

Resonance of Romance

Like a melody flowing free,
Your heartbeat sings a song to me.
Each note lingers in the air,
In this symphony, love laid bare.

With every glance, a chord is struck,
In hushed tones, we share our luck.
The rhythm of life, we create,
In this dance, we celebrate fate.

Whispers of love, sweet serenades,
Echo softly through twilight shades.
In this embrace, our spirits soar,
Resonating forevermore.

Tangled hearts, a perfect rhyme,
In each moment, we freeze time.
With you, my love, I feel so free,
In this romance, it’s you and me.

As stars sparkle in the night,
Our love’s reflection, pure and bright.
In the silence, our thoughts align,
In this sonnet, you’re forever mine.

The Scene of Our Souls

In the twilight, shadows play,
As our worries fade away.
A soft breeze whispers our tale,
In the moment, we will prevail.

Eyes like starlight, deep and clear,
Every heartbeat a promise near.
In the silence, our souls unite,
Painting dreams in the soft moonlight.

With laughter bright, we paint the day,
In our haven, we find a way.
Together, we face all our fears,
Sharing laughter, sharing tears.

Two spirits bound in endless gleam,
Chasing horizons, living the dream.
Every second, each gentle sigh,
In this scene, we learn to fly.

With hands held tight, we wander far,
Guided always by love's bright star.
In the canvas of time, we unfold,
The scene of our souls, a story told.

Captivated by You

In silence, your gaze holds me tight,
In your presence, the world feels right.
Each moment shared, a spark ignites,
Captivated by love's gentle lights.

With every laugh, the stars align,
In your smile, I see the divine.
The beauty in simple things,
Captivated by what true love brings.

In the whispers of the night sky,
With you, my dear, we learn to fly.
Every heartbeat a cherished song,
In your arms, where I belong.

As seasons change, our roots grow deep,
In shared dreams, we sow and reap.
Together we weave life's rich hue,
Captivated by the essence of you.

Through life's journey, hand in hand,
In this dance, we take our stand.
Forever bonded, forever true,
In this love, I'm captivated by you.

The Beauty Between Us

In whispers soft, our secrets shared,
A bond unbroken, hearts laid bare.
Through storms and sun, we find our way,
The beauty blooms in bright array.

With every glance, the world ignites,
In silent dances, our souls unite.
Together we weave a tapestry,
Of love and light, pure harmony.

Your laughter rings like gentle chimes,
In perfect sync, across space and times.
With every step, we paint the sky,
A canvas bright, no need to try.

Through trials faced, we stand as one,
In shadows cast, our light begun.
With hands entwined, we forge ahead,
In every word, love's truth is spread.

So here we stand, side by side,
In this vast world, our hearts abide.
A radiant dawn, where dreams take flight,
The beauty between us, purest light.

Mosaics of Emotion

Each shattered piece, a story told,
In colors bright, the heart unfolds.
From joy to sorrow, laughter, pain,
A vivid dance, in every grain.

Fragments scattered, yet intertwined,
In chaos, beauty we can find.
With gentle hands, we mend the past,
Creating art, meant to last.

Rich hues collide, in vibrant sway,
As memories blend in bright array.
Layers deep, the heart does trust,
Mosaics made from love and dust.

In every crack, a glimpse of grace,
In tears we find our sacred space.
Together crafting what we feel,
A masterpiece that helps to heal.

So let us build, with love's design,
A world where hearts and colors shine.
In every piece, a truth, a dream,
Mosaics of emotion, a flowing stream.

Echoes of Euphoria

In fleeting moments, shadows play,
An evening glow, the end of day.
With laughter ringing through the air,
Echoes dance, without a care.

A heartbeat quickens, time stands still,
In perfect harmony, we feel the thrill.
With every smile, a spark ignites,
A flame of joy that brings delight.

With hands outstretched, we chase the light,
In every whisper, love takes flight.
Through laughter, tears, we find our way,
Echoes of euphoria lead the sway.

A melody that never fades,
In every note, a memory cascades.
Through shared adventures, dreams unfurl,
In this sweet bliss, we find our world.

So let us leap, embrace the rush,
In tender moments, feel the hush.
With every heartbeat, let us sing,
Echoes of euphoria take wing.

Reflected Embrace

In twilight's glow, we find our space,
Two souls entwined in a warm embrace.
As shadows blend and colors fade,
In mirrored depths, love is portrayed.

Through whispered dreams, we journey far,
Guided gently by a shining star.
In moments shared, we hold what's true,
Reflected light, me and you.

With every sigh, a memory holds,
In tender warmth, our story unfolds.
Through every storm, we find our peace,
In each embrace, the world’s release.

So take my hand, let’s dance the night,
In every step, find pure delight.
Together here, we’ll weave our tale,
Reflected love that will not pale.

In quiet nights, let hearts confide,
In every pulse, our hopes abide.
Through life's embrace, we rise, we glow,
Reflected love, forever flow.

Reflections of Affection

In the quiet of the night,
Whispers softly arise,
Hearts dance in the shadows,
Beneath the starlit skies.

A touch that speaks of trust,
Fingers interlaced,
Moments wrapped in warmth,
In love's gentle embrace.

Every laugh a melody,
Every sigh a song,
In your gaze, I find peace,
Where my heart belongs.

Memories softly woven,
Threads of golden light,
In the tapestry of us,
Love shines ever bright.

Time stands still with you,
As hours gently fade,
In reflections of affection,
A bond that won’t evade.

Through Heart's Prism

Colors blend and swirl,
In the depths of the soul,
Every hue a heartbeat,
In love, we find our role.

Through heart's prism we see,
The world in vivid shades,
Every glance a spectrum,
In each silence, cascades.

Laughter dances brightly,
A symphony of light,
Every word a heartbeat,
In the laughter of night.

Moments captured softly,
In stillness intertwined,
Through heart's prism we find,
The beauty of our minds.

In every hue, a promise,
In every shade, a dream,
Through heart's prism we travel,
Together, we shall gleam.

Shades of Adoration

In the dawn's tender glow,
Adoration takes its flight,
Each glance a silent vow,
In the soft morning light.

Whispers shared on the breeze,
Secrets only we know,
In shades of adoration,
Our love begins to grow.

Through trials and through triumphs,
Hand in hand, we will stand,
In the colors of our journey,
We create our own land.

With laughter sprinkled bright,
And love's gentle embrace,
In shades of adoration,
We find our perfect space.

Forever in this moment,
In the beauty that we weave,
Shades of love will guide us,
In each heart, we believe.

In the Clarity of Emotion

Through the fog of confusion,
Your gaze cuts like a knife,
In the clarity of emotion,
I discover true life.

With every tear we've shed,
And laughter shared in jest,
In the clarity of emotion,
We find what feels the best.

The world can fade away,
When you're here by my side,
In the clarity of emotion,
Our hearts will be our guide.

Moments crystallized,
In the warmth of your touch,
In the clarity of emotion,
I find I need you much.

So hand in hand, we'll walk,
Through storms and sunny skies,
In the clarity of emotion,
True love never dies.

When Hearts Align

In the hush of twilight's glow,
Two souls intertwine, soft and slow.
With whispers shared beneath the stars,
Love blossoms bright, despite the scars.

Paths once lonely now intertwine,
Every heartbeat, a gentle sign.
In the dance of fate, they find their way,
Dreams woven close, night turns to day.

With every glance, the world fades away,
In this moment, time dares not sway.
Together they rise, unbroken, strong,
In the silence, they find their song.

Through trials faced and storms endured,
Their bond, a treasure, pure and assured.
When hearts align, fate holds them tight,
Together, they chase the endless light.

Lenses of Tenderness

In the quiet gaze of tender eyes,
A universe unfolds beneath the skies.
Moments captured like fragile glass,
Through lenses of love, memories amass.

The world, a canvas painted anew,
With vibrant hues where hearts break through.
Each smile exchanged, a painted stroke,
In the silence, their laughter spoke.

Shadows dance where light touches ground,
In sweet reflections, hope is found.
Through trials, the lens grows ever clear,
Every heartbeat sings, “I am here.”

Together they see through love’s embrace,
In this fleeting moment, they find their place.
With every glance, with every sigh,
Through lenses of tenderness, they fly.

Kaleidoscope of Souls

Within the dance of colors bright,
Souls intertwine in pure delight.
In a kaleidoscope, they spin and sway,
Dreaming of love in a vibrant array.

Fragments of laughter, shards of pain,
Together they weather the pouring rain.
In the prism of trust, they bloom and grow,
A beautiful chaos in love's warm glow.

Through each revolution, they find their way,
Creating patterns that always stay.
In every heartbeat, a story told,
In the art of love, they are bold.

When worlds collide and passions ignite,
In the kaleidoscope, all feels right.
A tapestry woven, hearts forever bound,
In this dance of souls, true love is found.

Distorted Realities of Romance

In shadows cast by doubt's cruel hand,
Love’s reflection seems to shift and bend.
Each whispered promise floats in the air,
Yet tangled truths weave a thread of despair.

Through a mirror cracked, they seek the light,
Fearing the echoes of a long, lost fight.
Yet in the chaos, sparks start to glow,
Distorted realities begin to show.

In the labyrinth of pain, they navigate,
Searching for solace amidst the hate.
With every turn, hope flickers in flight,
In the midst of the storm, they find their might.

Love's shattered pieces begin to align,
Creating beauty from the decline.
In the heart's embrace, they find their own,
Though fractured, together, never alone.

Lens of Longing

In shadows cast by fading light,
The heart seeks what is out of sight.
A glimpse of dreams, a whisper clear,
Through the lens, we draw you near.

Each moment captured, frozen still,
A story told against the chill.
We filter truth through veils of hope,
In longing's grasp, we learn to cope.

Reflections dance in twilight's glow,
A bittersweet, familiar flow.
We search for what we once have missed,
In every frame, a haunting twist.

A canvas wide, with colors bright,
We pen our tales, igniting night.
Through sorrow's lens, through joy's embrace,
Each tear and smile, a sacred space.

Within our gaze, the world transforms,
New paths emerge, the heart informs.
With every click, we seize the chance,
To weave our tales in life's vast dance.

Tinted Memories

Faded images whisper the past,
Each frame a tale, forever cast.
In sepia tones, emotions bleed,
Tinted visions fulfill our need.

We sift through time, the dust of days,
Awash in the warmth of golden rays.
Moments linger, sweet yet brief,
In memories held, we find relief.

Echoes of laughter, soft and clear,
Each snapshot holds what we hold dear.
With every glance, a story spins,
A tapestry woven of losses and wins.

Between the frames, the heartbeats play,
The light softens, guiding the gray.
We cherish the hues that paint our days,
In tinted moments, love still stays.

A bittersweet blend of joy and pain,
In every tear, a fragile chain.
We honor the past, embrace what's real,
In tinted memories, we deeply feel.

Framing Love's Unfolding

Through the lens, our story blooms,
In quiet rooms, where the heart consumes.
Each glance a brush, each smile a stroke,
We frame the love in words unbroke.

In the soft light of gentle dawn,
We capture moments, forever drawn.
With every blink, new dreams arise,
In the canvas of her eyes.

Whispers of hope, in shadows deep,
In the sacred trust, our secrets keep.
With every frame that time bestows,
Love's essence thrives, as passion grows.

We sculpt the air with tender grace,
Carved in laughter, no need to erase.
In corners bright, where shadows dance,
Our love unfolds, a sweet romance.

Through stormy skies and sunlit bliss,
Each click of time, each fleeting kiss.
In every heartbeat, our truth takes flight,
Framing love, in day and night.

Embracing the Light

In twilight's glow, we find our peace,
Each golden ray, a warm release.
With open arms, we greet the dawn,
Embracing light, our fears are gone.

A dance of shadows, bright and bold,
We weave our dreams in threads of gold.
In soft reflection, we learn to see,
The beauty in the dark sets us free.

The heart beats deep with every sigh,
In the arms of light, we learn to fly.
Moments like fire, fierce and bright,
Igniting hope, dispelling night.

Together we stand, hand in hand,
In the language of love, we understand.
With every heartbeat, the world aligns,
In light's embrace, our spirit shines.

A journey woven in sun's warm rays,
In tender echoes of our days.
With every sunrise, love's promise gleams,
Embracing the light, we chase our dreams.

Panoramic Whispers

Whispers dance across the sky,
Carrying secrets, low and high.
Mountains stand with ancient grace,
While rivers flow in a warm embrace.

Stars gather in a silent thrill,
Echoes linger, time stands still.
Each heartbeat paints a vivid scene,
In this landscape, calm and serene.

Fog rolls in like a gentle sheet,
Concealing paths where wanderers meet.
Leaves rustle in the evening breeze,
Nature’s sound, a soothing tease.

The sun dips low, a fiery burst,
Lighting skies with colors rehearsed.
Horizons stretch, a canvas grand,
Life's symphony at our command.

With every glance, a story unfolds,
In panoramic views, courage molds.
Together we tread this ethereal floor,
Finding peace forevermore.

A Clear View to the Heart

Gazing deep through crystal glass,
I find the truths that shadows pass.
In reflections, emotions sway,
A mirror of our joyous play.

Moments frozen in quiet frames,
Whispers linger, igniting flames.
Hearts unite with every glance,
In this dance, we take our chance.

Simplicity holds a radiant glow,
In the warmth, our spirits flow.
With open windows, let love beam,
A clear view within, a cherished dream.

Underneath the starlit sky,
Promises soar, and hopes comply.
In a heartbeat, our souls entwine,
To see the heart, it's simply divine.

A canvas painted in vivid hues,
Each emotion, bright and true.
Life unfolds with gentle art,
In this clear view to the heart.

Moments in the Spectrum

Colors swirl in vibrant light,
Each hue whispering day and night.
Moments captured in every shade,
Life’s palette, beautifully laid.

Crimson drapes the evening sky,
As dreams awaken, desires fly.
Golden rays break the dawn,
Hope ignites as shadows yawn.

Beneath the azure, spirits blend,
Time flows with a gentle bend.
In electric greens, laughter blooms,
Echoing joy in crowded rooms.

Indigo flows like a soothing stream,
Carrying memories, light as a dream.
Moments layer in twilight's embrace,
Painting life’s grand, vibrant space.

In every heartbeat, colors arise,
Telling tales through the silent skies.
We celebrate each fleeting scene,
Moments in the spectrum, serene.

Colors of Connection

In every glance, a bond is formed,
Two souls dancing, hearts warmed.
Scarlet threads intertwine tight,
Leading us toward the light.

Ocean blue speaks of our trust,
In harmonious whispers, we find us.
Mellow yellows, laughter shared,
In every moment, love declared.

Emerald fields stretch far and wide,
Embracing journeys side by side.
Together we paint our vivid dreams,
In the colors of connection, it seems.

Golden sunsets embrace the night,
A tapestry of pure delight.
With every step, we're intertwined,
In colors that time won't unwind.

The spectrum shines as we explore,
In every heartbeat, we crave more.
With every shared moment, we thrive,
Coloring our world, alive.

The Viewfinder of Life

In a world so vast and wide,
We frame our moments inside.
Each snapshot tells a tale,
Of joy, of love, beyond the pale.

The light that plays across our face,
Time captured in a fleeting space.
With every click, a story born,
Of laughter shared, of hearts reborn.

Through lenses clear, we seek to find,
The beauty that unites mankind.
In shadows deep, or sunlit glow,
Life's viewfinder starts to show.

Memories stored within the frame,
Remind us all we're not the same.
Yet in the frame, we stand as one,
Together shining in the sun.

With each new frame, we learn to see,
The threads of love that bind you and me.
In life’s vast gallery, we thrive,
Forever captured, still alive.

Portraits of Intimacy

In the soft glow of candlelight,
Fingers brush with pure delight.
Whispers dance upon the air,
Love laid bare, a vibrant flare.

Eyes that speak, words left unsaid,
In these moments, hearts are fed.
With strokes of passion, we reveal,
The depth of warmth that love can heal.

A gaze that lingers, tender, deep,
In silence shared, promises we keep.
Together framed, a timeless art,
Each portrait speaks of a beating heart.

Ebb and flow like the tides of time,
Our souls entwined in perfect rhyme.
Every heartbeat, every sigh,
Captures love's sweet lullaby.

In shadows cast, in the evening light,
Two souls converge, the world ignites.
In portraits drawn with love's own hand,
We find our truth, we take our stand.

In the Focus of Emotion

Beyond the eyes, emotions gleam,
Each blink reveals another dream.
In laughter bright or brimming tears,
Life's focus sharpens through the years.

A tender smile, a fleeting glance,
In every moment, there's a dance.
The heart beats loud in quiet spaces,
In love's embrace, our time erases.

Joy spills over like morning light,
As we find solace in the night.
Beneath the surface, currents flow,
In the depths, true feelings grow.

With every heartbeat, we align,
In the focus of love's design.
A world unveiled in vibrant hues,
With every choice, we deeply choose.

And though the storms may come and go,
In the focus, we learn to grow.
With clear intent, we journey on,
In the depths of bonds, we’re never alone.

Depths of Delight

In twilight's kiss, we find our place,
Where laughter echoes, filled with grace.
Our hearts collide, a sweet embrace,
In the depths, we trace our space.

With every smile, we dive anew,
Discovering worlds in shades of blue.
The thrill of life, the joy of chance,
In moments shared, the heart's romance.

Each whispered secret, softly spun,
In the depths, our souls are one.
Through winding paths, we choose to roam,
In every step, we build our home.

The depths reveal what's pure and bright,
A canvas painted with delight.
With every breath, we learn to see,
The beauty found in you and me.

In laughter's echo, and tears we've shed,
In the depths of joy, we're truly led.
In love's embrace, our spirits soar,
Together in delight, forevermore.

Blurred Boundaries of Affection

In whispers soft, we dare to tread,
Where boundaries fade, and fears are shed.
Hearts entangle in the twilight glow,
Between the lines, our feelings flow.

Eyes that linger, a silent plea,
In the spaces where we long to be.
Fleeting moments, captured in dreams,
Love is woven in fragile seams.

Threads of laughter, sorrow's embrace,
In the blurred lines, we find our place.
Each heartbeat echoes, a gentle tune,
In the depths of night, beneath the moon.

An uncharted path we walk anew,
With hands entwined, we'll see it through.
A canvas painted in shades of grace,
With every glance, we find our space.

This dance of souls, both wild and free,
In love's embrace, we cease to be.
What once was separate, now is whole,
Blurred boundaries define our soul.

Lens of Vulnerability

Through a lens of truth, we stand exposed,
In moments raw, our hearts have dozed.
Fragile whispers on a winter's breeze,
Unveiling fears with such delicate ease.

A mirror’s gaze, revealing scars,
In softest shadows, love heals the bars.
With every tear that falls like rain,
We gather strength from shared pain.

In the quiet spaces, trust ignites,
Like stars that shimmer on velvet nights.
With open hearts and willing hands,
We craft a bond, no one understands.

Embracing flaws that make us whole,
The beauty found in our shared soul.
In the lens of vulnerability's grace,
We find our worth in each other's embrace.

Two hearts collide in a moment divine,
Finding solace in love’s sacred shrine.
In this transparency, we are reborn,
Building a world on trust, adorned.

Your Light, My Prism

In your glow, I find my spark,
A radiant flame that ignites the dark.
You shimmer bright, a guiding star,
Each beam of hope takes me far.

Colors dance in the evening sky,
With every laugh, we lift up high.
Your light bends in the softest way,
Casting rainbows on lonely days.

With every word, you shade my fear,
My heart awakens when you are near.
In the spectrum of love, we define,
The beauty in the space between our lines.

We build the world with glimmers bright,
In every heartache, you are my light.
Together we paint with colors unseen,
In the canvas of dreams, you reign supreme.

So shine, dear heart, for I'll find my place,
In your brilliance, I discover grace.
In this dance beneath skies so vast,
Your light is my prism, forever to last.

Visions Woven in Tenderness

In dreams we share, our hearts align,
A tapestry of love, so divine.
Every thread spun from hopes so bright,
We craft our world in the softest light.

With gentle whispers, we draw near,
In this cocoon, we shed each fear.
Visions blossom like flowers in bloom,
Filling our hearts with sweet perfume.

In every sigh, there's a promise made,
In tender moments, our worries fade.
We build a sanctuary, warm and safe,
Where love's reflection becomes our grace.

Each heartbeat echoes a lasting song,
Together, where we know we belong.
With outstretched hands and open minds,
In our closeness, true beauty finds.

With every dawn, new visions arise,
Woven in tenderness, a love that ties.
In the fabric of time, we craft our bliss,
In the heart's embrace, we find our kiss.

The Vibration of Hearts

In silence whispers softly breathe,
The rhythm of our hearts a woven sheath.
With every pulse, our stories entwine,
In the sacred dance, your soul meets mine.

A gentle touch beneath the stars,
Beyond the universe, we are not far.
In this embrace, time finds its pause,
Two hearts beating, just because.

Echoes linger in the soft night air,
Each heartbeat whispers, 'I am here, I care.'
Vibrations travel far and wide,
In this connection, we cannot hide.

As dawn breaks, the world awakes,
But in the quiet, the love still aches.
For in the stillness, we'll forever stay,
Vibration of hearts, guiding our way.

Together we rise, and together we fall,
In this cosmic journey, we conquer all.
With every heartbeat, we shall impart,
The unshakable bond of two vibrant hearts.

Contrast of Affection

In a world painted black and white,
Your love brings color, pure delight.
The warmth of sun against the rain,
In every contrast, joy and pain.

Soft whispers clash with echoing cries,
A tapestry woven of truth and lies.
Each moment cherished, every glance shared,
In the realm of affection, we are dared.

The sharpness of night meets the softness of day,
Every bitter note leads to a sweet ballet.
In laughter's spark and sorrow's guise,
The contrast of affection builds our ties.

Fleeting moments, yet etched in time,
A rhythm of hearts, a tender rhyme.
Together we stand, both fierce and meek,
Finding strength in what makes us unique.

In shadows cast, in light’s embrace,
We navigate love’s intricate space.
For every tear and every smile,
The contrast of affection stretches a mile.

Infinite Reflections

In mirrors held, we see our truth,
A dance of ages, reclaiming youth.
Every glance reveals a story told,
Infinite reflections, bright and bold.

In waters deep, we search our souls,
Within the ripples, time unfolds.
Each fragment shines a different hue,
In this reflection, I find you.

The kaleidoscope spins, colors blend,
In the circle of life, we transcend.
Round and round, our visions meet,
Infinite paths beneath our feet.

As light cascades upon the glass,
We witness moments as they pass.
In every echo, in every dream,
Reflections whisper, so it seems.

Through every challenge, every cheer,
In the fabric of fate, you draw near.
Infinite reflections guide our way,
Crafting our love, day by day.

The Frames We Build

In frames of trust, we craft our art,
Every corner whispers, a brand new start.
With each moment, we carefully mold,
A beautiful tapestry, stories unfold.

The foundation strong, built with care,
In laughter and tears, together we dare.
Every nail is a promise made,
In the frames we build, our hearts displayed.

Through shadows and light, our vision aligns,
With every brushstroke, love defines.
In the gallery of dreams, we'll reside,
In the frames we build, side by side.

As seasons shift and years drift away,
These memories linger, come what may.
Within each frame, our spirits soar,
In the life we create, we cherish more.

Together we paint, together we frame,
In this journey of hearts, nothing's the same.
Holding the dreams, as future calls,
In the frames we build, love conquers all.

Through the Glass of Yearning

In the stillness of night, I dream,
Reflections whisper soft and warm.
Each glance a silent, fragile beam,
Drawing me close to your charm.

The moon seems like your gentle smile,
Stars twinkle with your tender gaze.
I drift in thoughts, though miles compile,
Yearning through a silver haze.

In every shadow, your echo calls,
Haunting the corners of my mind.
Time gently flows, as memory stalls,
In longing's grasp, I'm intertwined.

Yet dawn breaks with its golden light,
Painting dreams in shades of hope.
Through the glass, I see our flight,
Together, we shall learn to cope.

So here I stand, my heart exposed,
In the depths of yearning's grasp.
With every glance, love's truth disclosed,
Our destinies in soft embrace clasp.

Colors of the Beloved

In the garden where whispers bloom,
Petals dance in soft embrace.
Each hue a brush, dispelling gloom,
Colors weave your timeless grace.

Blues reflect the calm of seas,
Reds ignite the fire within.
Greens echo the rustling breeze,
Drawing me to the love we spin.

Golden rays caress your face,
In sunlight's glow, you brightly sing.
Every moment, a painted place,
In my heart, you're everything.

Violet dreams drift through the air,
Whispers soft, like petals fall.
In each shade, your essence fair,
Colors of love, vibrant call.

Together we create our scene,
Crafting life with every stroke.
With hearts entwined, forever keen,
In your light, my spirit woke.

Embracing the Moment

The clock ticks slow, yet time stands still,
In every heartbeat, moments blend.
With open arms, I seek the thrill,
Embracing now, as time ascends.

In laughter shared and smiles exchanged,
Every second, a treasure found.
In vivid hues, our lives arranged,
The world around us, softly drowned.

Let go of worries, let them fade,
In this space, we breathe as one.
Life's canvas stretches, unafraid,
As daylight meets the setting sun.

Here we twirl in life's sweet dance,
With every glance, we spark anew.
Each moment, a fleeting chance,
Revealing dreams that once we knew.

So tethered close, let’s cherish time,
In pockets of joy, forever sway.
In whispers low, our souls entwined,
Embracing now, come what may.

The Portrait of Us

Two figures framed in softened light,
Brush strokes whisper tales untold.
In every glance, a shared delight,
Our journey painted, bright and bold.

With laughter etched upon the canvas,
Memories swirl in vivid hue.
The essence of love, a fine embalmus,
Each chapter reveals something new.

Hands interlaced, stories unfold,
Colors blend in perfect flair.
In the silence, our hearts behold,
A masterpiece beyond compare.

Time may weather the surface gloss,
But beneath lies a love so true.
In the portrait, no line is lost,
Each detail speaks of me and you.

Together we sit, side by side,
Harmonies echo from heart to heart.
In every shadow, love's abide,
The portrait lives, we're never apart.

Through Sheen and Shadow

In the twilight's gentle glow,
Whispers dance on quiet air.
Lost within the ebb and flow,
Hearts entwined, a secret flare.

Shadows stretch like softened sighs,
Veils of dreams that softly wane.
Truth resides in muted eyes,
Yearning waltz, a sweet refrain.

Through the mist, the world ignites,
Flickers warm with ghostly light.
Every breath a chance to find,
Beauty woven in the night.

Silent echoes fill the space,
Time dissolves into a stream.
Hand in hand, we softly trace,
Moments spun from whispered dream.

In the sheen, a promise glows,
Every shadow speaks of time.
Here's where love forever grows,
In the dark, the heart will climb.

Capturing Fleeting Glances

A fleeting look, a passing smile,
The world slows down for just a beat.
In that moment, time's worthwhile,
Hearts collide, embrace the heat.

Eyes like stars that twinkle bright,
Drawing souls with gentle grace.
Every glance ignites the night,
A dance that time cannot erase.

Words unsaid, the silence speaks,
Secrets bloom in every gaze.
Through the chaos, love still seeks,
Light that lingers in a haze.

Capturing dreams that slip away,
Caught in tides of passing chance.
Heartbeats quicken, come what may,
In each glance, a wild romance.

Moments fade as shadows shift,
Yet the echoes softly stay.
In our hearts, a cherished gift,
Memories that light the way.

Vision of Sweet Surrender

In a realm of whispered dreams,
Sweet surrender calls our name.
Through the void, the starlight beams,
Love unfolds with soft acclaim.

Steps entwined, our paths aligned,
Every heartbeat writes a tune.
In your eyes, the stars are mined,
Guiding us beneath the moon.

With each breath, we push the tide,
Fleeting moments hold us tight.
In this flow, our hearts abide,
Lost in love's eternal light.

Tender whispers, gentle sighs,
Unraveled by the night's caress.
In your arms, where freedom lies,
Time's sweet hold is but a stress.

Captured in this dance of grace,
Passing shadows fade away.
In surrender, find our place,
Love, the vision that will stay.

The Beauty of Nearness

In the tangled threads of fate,
Our hands brush, a spark ignites.
Every moment feels so great,
Whispered dreams in soft delights.

Closer now, we share our breath,
A warmth that softens every word.
In this space, we find no death,
Life blooms bright and unperturbed.

Eyes meet eyes, the world dissolves,
Vows exchanged in secret air.
With each second, love evolves,
Deepened ties, no need for flair.

All around, the chaos fades,
In this realm, we find our peace.
Every fear and doubt cascades,
As our hearts begin to lease.

The beauty of our near embrace,
Holds the universe within.
In this love, we find our place,
A journey where our souls begin.

The Essence of Togetherness

In laughter, we find our place,
Hand in hand, hearts embrace.
Through storms, we stand so tall,
Together, we conquer all.

In silence, our souls unite,
In the dark, you are my light.
Through whispers, our fears arise,
In your gaze, no need for lies.

Each moment, shared like a song,
In this bond, we both belong.
With joys and sorrows we share,
In the journey, love laid bare.

Through seasons of change, we grow,
In the warmth of love's glow.
Together, our spirits dance,
In the magic of each chance.

The essence of us shines bright,
In our hearts, a guiding light.
Forever, we'll stand the test,
In togetherness, we are blessed.

Focal Points of Love

In your smile, I feel the spark,
Guiding me through the dark.
With each touch, a gentle sway,
In our hearts, love finds a way.

With every glance, a shared dream,
In your eyes, I see the gleam.
With tender words, we craft the day,
In silence, our feelings stay.

Through moments, both big and small,
In your presence, I stand tall.
With laughter that fills the air,
In this love, we find our care.

Each heartbeat is a silent vow,
In the now, we find our how.
With every step, a dance anew,
In our love, we live so true.

The focal points of our embrace,
In this life, we find our place.
With every memory we weave,
In love, we shall always believe.

Infinity in a Single Frame

In a glance, the world stands still,
Captured moments, hearts fulfill.
With your smile that lights the way,
In stillness, words fail to say.

Through the lens, our lives unfold,
In every story, love is told.
With every click, a memory made,
In our hearts, the fears do fade.

A snapshot of joy and grace,
In your arms, a warm embrace.
Through the chaos, you're my peace,
In this frame, our love won't cease.

Moments freeze, yet time moves on,
In this dance, we are the song.
With every beat, our souls align,
In this frame, forever shine.

Infinity captured, we exist,
In our love, a perfect twist.
With every brush of fate's hand,
In this frame, we understand.

Radiant Reflections

In the mirror, I see your glow,
Radiance that we both know.
Through reflections, our love takes flight,
In the shadows, you are my light.

With every glance, a story shared,
In every moment, we have dared.
Through struggles, we rise above,
In every challenge, shines our love.

With colors that blend and swirl,
In this life, you are my pearl.
Every laugh, a burst of sun,
In our hearts, we are as one.

Through the seasons, joy persists,
In our dreams, love still exists.
With every heartbeat, visions bright,
In this journey, pure delight.

Radiant reflections, a tapestry spun,
In the warmth of two, we are one.
With every memory we create,
In love, we find our fate.

Shades of Enchantment

In the dusky light, shadows play,
Whispers of dreams that quietly sway.
Colors collide in a gentle embrace,
Each hue reveals a secret place.

Stars flicker softly in velvet skies,
Tales of magic in sparkling eyes.
Moonlight dances on the lake's serene,
Reflecting wonders, both pure and keen.

Nature's rhythm, a soft, sweet tune,
Breezes carry scents of blooming June.
Petals unfold in a quiet sigh,
Breathing life as the night drifts by.

In the twilight, enchantment sings,
Where hope is born and freedom clings.
Every shadow whispers a tale,
In the heart where dreams prevail.

A tapestry woven with memories bright,
Captured moments in the soft moonlight.
Here, in the stillness, we find our way,
In shades of enchantment, we long to stay.

In a Frame of Longing

Through a windowpane, I gaze afar,
Awash in thoughts of who you are.
Every fleeting moment feels like gold,
Whispers of stories yet untold.

Captured in time, a lingering glance,
Silent wishes sparking a chance.
In the shadows of my mind you dwell,
Echoing rhythms, a soft, sweet bell.

Frames of memory, both tender and bright,
Filling the heart with gentle light.
Longing thrives where silence grows,
In a symphony only the heart knows.

Fingers trace paths of embroidered dreams,
Flowing like rivers in moonlit streams.
Each petal of memory falls down,
Painting the silence, wearing a crown.

In this still world where wishes drift,
I hold the fragments, a precious gift.
In a frame of longing, hope does remain,
As love whispers softly, like gentle rain.

Vignettes of Us

Moments are photos etched in time,
Captured reflections, an endless rhyme.
In laughter shared, joy brightly glows,
In quiet corners, love gently grows.

Hand in hand, we wander the streets,
Life's melody plays, with heartbeats.
Every snapshot tells a sweet tale,
In the winds of memory, we shall sail.

Sunsets spark dreams we chase in flight,
Underneath stars, wrapped in the night.
Beneath the moon's soft, silvery cloak,
Our souls entwined, as the universe spoke.

Mosaic of moments, forever we weave,
In shadows of laughter, we dare to believe.
Every glance tells of love so deep,
Vignettes of us, in our hearts we keep.

In the tapestry of time, we unfold,
Stories of warmth, in whispers retold.
Together we stand, unyielding, free,
In vignettes of us, just you and me.

Mirage of Emotions

In the distance, a shimmer appears,
Echoes of hopes, drenched in fears.
Mirage of dreams, elusive and bright,
Dancing like flames in the dark of night.

Waves of feelings crash on the shore,
Each heartbeat whispers tales of lore.
In the silence, we seek to find,
The threads of longing that intertwine.

A fleeting glance, a touch, a sigh,
In the vast expanse, where shadows lie.
Emotions flicker like stars above,
Guiding us gently toward what we love.

Mirrors reflect what the heart conceals,
Stories of loss, or the joy it reveals.
In the depths of longing, we find our way,
Chasing the light of a brand new day.

With every heartbeat, we weave a song,
In a world where fragile dreams belong.
Mirage of emotions, a quest so true,
In the landscape of longing, I seek for you.

In the Capture of Moments

A whisper in the night, soft and clear,
A glance exchanged, pulling you near.
Time suspends, a heartbeat caught,
In fleeting seconds, we find what's sought.

The laughter shared, echoes of glee,
Painting memories, just you and me.
Each smile captured, a story unfolds,
In the frame of life, where warmth beholds.

Seasons change, yet still, we hold tight,
Every moment cherished, glowing bright.
In photographs taken, love's embrace,
In the art of now, we find our place.

With every sunset kissed by the day,
In fleeting moments, we find our way.
A dance of shadows, light plays along,
In the capture of moments, we find our song.

So let us gather each instant we find,
In the embrace of time, forever entwined.
Through laughter and tears, we'll always strive,
In the capture of moments, we truly thrive.

The Journey of Glances

A simple gaze, a map so surreal,
Leading hearts, revealing the real.
Every flicker holds a tale untold,
In the journey of glances, treasures unfold.

Through crowded rooms, our eyes collide,
A silent conversation, no need to hide.
Worlds intertwine, breaths shared anew,
In the journey of glances, I see you.

From fleeting looks, to moments shared,
In every heartbeat, love is declared.
A tapestry woven with threads of sight,
In the journey of glances, everything feels right.

With every stare, a spark ignites,
In shadows and light, the future invites.
Each connection a step toward what’s true,
In the journey of glances, it’s me and you.

So let us wander on this path dressed in light,
With eyes open wide, hearts bursting in flight.
In each fleeting look, let's embrace the chance,
In the journey of glances, we learn to dance.

Every Look a Treasure

In every look, a world awakens,
Fleeting moments, yet hearts unshaken.
Eyes like windows to souls we seek,
Every look a treasure, secrets unique.

Silent wishes dance in the air,
A glance that lingers, a promise laid bare.
With every flutter, a spark ignites,
In every look a treasure, the heart delights.

Through laughter, sorrows, all intertwined,
In the depths of gaze, our truths we find.
Like precious gems, these stolen stares,
In every look a treasure, love declares.

A silent language, whispers of fate,
In every fleeting glance, we create.
Moments captured, forever they last,
Every look a treasure, treasures amassed.

As time moves on, we'll still remember,
The warmth and light of each ember.
In the eyes of others, we'll always see,
Every look a treasure, you and me.

Emotions on Canvas

With every stroke, a feeling glows,
Colors dance, as the heart overflows.
Brush in hand, the canvas sighs,
Emotions painted in vibrant skies.

A palette rich with hopes and fears,
Layer by layer, unveiling tears.
In the blend of shades, our souls entwine,
Emotions on canvas, a world divine.

Each hue tells stories long left unsaid,
With every splash, a memory spread.
From the darkest nights to sunlit days,
Emotions on canvas, love's endless maze.

The art of feeling, captured with grace,
In every stroke, an embrace, a trace.
As colors merge, we find our way,
Emotions on canvas, come what may.

So let us paint what the heart can't hide,
In the splash of colors, truth will abide.
Together we'll create what time cannot sever,
Emotions on canvas, forever and ever.

A Glimpse of Harmony

In whispers soft the breezes play,
Carrying dreams of a brighter day.
Petals dance on the morning light,
As hope unfolds in gentle flight.

Mountains stand in quiet grace,
While rivers weave a soothing trace.
Nature sings in vibrant hues,
Filling souls with joyful news.

The sun dips low, a golden kiss,
Creating moments we cannot miss.
With every beat, the heart can feel,
A glimpse of beauty, warm and real.

In unity, we find our song,
Together we are, forever strong.
Hand in hand through twists and turns,
In harmony, our spirit burns.

Beneath the stars, the cosmos gleams,
In tranquil nights we share our dreams.
A tapestry of love unfolds,
In harmony, the world beholds.

Shadows of Sweetness

In twilight's blush, the shadows play,
Soft echoes of a fleeting day.
The dusk holds secrets yet untold,
As dreams and memories unfold.

Silhouettes in the moonlight gleam,
Whispers of warmth in every beam.
Underneath the silver sky,
Hearts awaken, hopes run high.

Gentle sighs in the evening air,
Fleeting moments, tender care.
As starlight kisses the silent ground,
In shadows, sweet love is found.

Among the branches, shadows dance,
Casting spells with a fleeting glance.
In every heartbeat, sweet release,
A symphony of softest peace.

Tomorrow waits with open arms,
For shadows guard our deepest charms.
In each embrace, the night reveals,
The sweetness that the heart conceals.

The Lens of Longing

Through windows wide, the world appears,
A canvas painted with our tears.
In every glance, the stories blend,
A longing heart that cannot mend.

Moments slip like grains of sand,
In distant lands, dreams stretch their hand.
The lens of longing captures sights,
Of starry skies and endless nights.

Where shadows whisper sweet refrain,
And every joy is paired with pain.
The heart beats loud, a rhythmic song,
In every sigh, where we belong.

Through every fog, the vision clears,
A path illuminated by our fears.
With hope ignited in the soul,
We chase the dreams that make us whole.

In every heartbeat lies the key,
Unlocking all that's meant to be.
Through the lens, we find our way,
In longing's grasp, we dare to stay.

Yet steadfast love shall light the dark,
Guiding hearts with its gentle spark.
In each reflection, we shall see,
The lens of longing setting free.

Captured Hearts

In silent hours, our spirits blend,
Two wandering souls that fate would send.
Captured moments in soft embrace,
Creating joy in this sacred space.

With laughter shared and stories spun,
Each heartbeats echo, two beats as one.
In tender glances, we come alive,
In every heartbeat, we truly thrive.

Through seasons' change, we stand as one,
In autumn’s glow or spring’s sweet sun.
Captured hearts in time's gentle flow,
Together we rise, together we grow.

In storms of life, we find our peace,
In love's warm light, our worries cease.
Bound by threads of joy and art,
Forever woven, captured hearts.

With every dawn, new dreams begin,
In this dance of life, we both win.
In whispered words and vows we hold,
Captured hearts, our love retold.

In the twilight's glow, our spirits soar,
A promise made, forevermore.
Together still, we'll chart our course,
In captured hearts, we find our force.

Through Rose-Colored Glasses

Life blooms softly in hues of pink,
Joy dances lightly, no time to think.
Glistening moments, bright and clear,
Held in the warmth, free from fear.

Each dawn whispers secrets anew,
Even the shadows, dressed in dew.
Hope trails behind, a gentle breeze,
Carrying dreams with effortless ease.

In laughter's echo, hearts entwine,
Every glance, a spark divine.
We see the world through tender sights,
The mundane transforms into delights.

Hand in hand, we wander wide,
Through fields of flowers, love our guide.
Casting aside the weight of gray,
Grateful for each golden ray.

With colors warm, we paint our days,
Lost in the softest of ways.
Through rose-colored glasses, we see,
The beauty in you, the beauty in me.

Heartstrings in Focus

A melody plays upon the breeze,
Stirring emotions, a gentle tease.
With every note, your laughter rings,
Tuning my heart to all the strings.

In twilight's glow, we take our place,
The world fades softly, time slows its race.
Moments captured in timeless frames,
Each glance ignites love's tender flames.

With whispers shared beneath the stars,
Every heartbeat heals old scars.
Intimate secrets carried away,
In the silence where our spirits sway.

Your heartbeat syncs with mine in tune,
Under the watch of a silver moon.
In this dance, we lose all doubt,
Through heartstrings in focus, love sings out.

Together we weave a vibrant thread,
In every word, a promise said.
Through life's rhythm, we'll find our way,
In our embrace, forever stay.

Spectrum of Affection

Colors swirl in a radiant dance,
With every glance, deepens romance.
From softest pastels to bright, bold hues,
Each shade a story, love's sweet muse.

In laughter stitched with threads of care,
A canvas bright, no need for spare.
With each heartbeat, we blend and mix,
Creating art that love depicts.

Captured moments in sunlit rays,
Even the simplest act conveys.
Together, we paint the skies above,
In the vibrant spectrum of our love.

When shadows creep and colors fade,
In your warmth, I have it made.
We find the beauty, rich and rare,
In every moment, love laid bare.

So let us wander, hand in hand,
Creating masterpieces, unplanned.
In the broad spectrum, bright and true,
This journey of affection, just me and you.

Fragments of Desire

In the quiet hush of evening's glow,
Whispers of longing gently flow.
Fragments of dreams, woven tight,
Chasing the stars, igniting the night.

Barefoot on grass, we chase the dawn,
Where shadows linger, and fears are gone.
With every heartbeat, our hopes ignite,
Desires unfurling, taking flight.

Fleeting moments, stolen glances,
In the silence, the heart romances.
Threads of affection, woven so fine,
In each fragment, your soul connects with mine.

A tapestry rich, stitched with care,
In every layer, memories share.
Binding us close with threads of fire,
Together we rise in fragments of desire.

So let us dance through the twilight's embrace,
In the spaces between, we find our place.
With every whisper and every sigh,
We'll gather the fragments, you and I.

In Focus: You and I

In quiet moments by your side,
The world fades into gentle hues,
With every glance, our hearts collide,
Creating stories that feel so new.

Your laughter dances on the breeze,
A melody that warms the soul,
In this space, we find our ease,
Together, we are truly whole.

Through shared whispers, secrets bloom,
In every gaze, a spark ignites,
We navigate the dusk and gloom,
Hand in hand, we chase the lights.

With you, the colors start to blend,
A canvas rich with dreams we paint,
Here in our world, we'll never bend,
For love like ours is far from faint.

So let us stay in this embrace,
Where visions of us intertwine,
In every moment, find our place,
In focus, forever you are mine.

Chasing the Soft Light

As dawn awakes with golden sighs,
We wander where the shadows play,
Chasing the soft light in the skies,
Finding magic in the day.

The warmth upon your gentle skin,
A glow that lights the paths we roam,
In silence, lovesongs softly spin,
In every step, we're close to home.

With every moment, time stands still,
The soft light casts a gentle hue,
Together, navigating will,
With dreams that shimmer, bright and true.

Through fields of hope, our spirits soar,
Each heartbeat echoes, wild and free,
In chasing light, we want for more,
Together in this symphony.

So let us dance until it's night,
With stars above, our hearts entwined,
In every flicker, pure delight,
In chasing the soft light, you're mine.

Visions of Us Together

In every dream, there you reside,
A vision clear, a heartbeat strong,
With you, my soul cannot divide,
In this journey, we belong.

Through whispered hopes and soft goodbyes,
We weave our tales with threads of gold,
In laughter shared and joyful sighs,
Our love's a story yet untold.

Each moment captured in your gaze,
Reflects a future bright and bold,
Within this sweet and endless haze,
A promise brighter than pure gold.

As shadows fall, our dreams take flight,
In visions painted with your smile,
We'll navigate through day and night,
In every step, we'll close the mile.

For in this dance, we find our place,
A rhythm that the stars align,
In visions of us, time can't erase,
Forever yours, forever mine.

Reflections in a Radiant Frame

In quiet corners, we both stand,
Reflections caught in gentle light,
Held within a steady hand,
Mirrored moments, pure delight.

Each glance a portal to the past,
Where laughter echoes in the glass,
In every shimmer, shadows cast,
We find the joy that seems to last.

With every frame, a tale unfolds,
Of love that deepens with each day,
In radiant hues, our story molds,
Capturing the dreams that lead the way.

Through golden sunsets, we will roam,
In reflections of what we create,
The world becomes our cherished home,
As time, in stillness, holds our fate.

So let us savor every glance,
In frames of warmth and soft embrace,
For every moment holds the chance,
To find ourselves in time and space.

Milton Keynes UK
Ingram Content Group UK Ltd.
UKHW022049111124
451035UK00014B/1020

9 789916 866009